Matt Abbott

Two Little Ducks
(and Selected Poems 2015-2018)

VERVE
POETRY PRESS
BIRMINGHAM

PUBLISHED BY VERVE POETRY PRESS
Birmingham, West Midlands, UK
https://vervepoetrypress.com
mail@vervepoetrypress.com

FIRST PUBLISHED OCT 2018

Printed and bound in the UK
by TJ International, Padstow

Cover heavily based on original designs by Mark Coverdale

ISBN: 978-1-912565-06-1

This collection is dedicated to three women.

My mum, Jan – the great enabler since day zero.

My partner, Maria – for whom I now have liquor on my Pie & Mash instead of gravy (but only down south).

And my dear friend Tracey, who passed away in 2012.
"We're here for a good time, not a long time".

CONTENTS

Foreword by Salena Godden

(ii)   *Selected Poems 2015-2018*

FOREWORD

It is with great pleasure that I write this foreword. Writing this, I feel like I have the honour of introducing you to a brilliant friend - someone I'm proud to call a friend - and a poet I admire very much. It is wonderful to see the poetry of Matt Abbott collected here in print. This is vital and deliberate work, observant poetry crafted with tenderness, wit, grit and precision.

Being a full-time poet is a peculiar and ridiculous ride of highs and lows and ins and outs. Ever since I have known Matt he has shared this fantastic positive energy, enthusiasm and vision. He has well and truly paid his dues time and time again. Matt Abbott is the real deal. He isn't just a writer of poems - he isn't just a performer either. He is an avid reader, a poetry supporter and because of this, this love of the art-form shows, it shines, the work leaps off the pages.

When Matt first appeared on my radar he was already well on his way. He was already running his own poetry label Nymphs and Thugs. He was sharing and contributing to the poetry community, organising and promoting regular events and zines. Plus donating his time and energy to work for charities and teaching workshops, as well as finessing his craft, his writing and performance work too. And the results we have here in this book are a manifestation of all of that dedication and hard work.

So here's the proof. You have in your hands Matt Abbott's first full poetry collection. It is steeped in his kindness and generosity. I also feel there is an urgency to this work. I feel this book is a rallying cry. I think this is an important collection for us and for the here and now.

These pieces of Matt's depict and decipher real struggle, real life lived, real stories, all with working class soul. This work has got its hands dirty and it's face filthy. Reading this I'm transported through history and geography. I envision poverty, raw and humble hungers, intertwined with present day turmoil and horror. These poems show us the bare roots of the UK's triumphs and failures, the problems we share now or have seen and bear witness to - our own prejudices, fear and intolerance.

There are deadly serious tones in this collection - there is real punch and kick in here. This work does not shy away from the bold, brutal and beautiful truth. However where there are shadows, there is such deft work with light, with hope, and on every page so much heart. It's a real joy to read and an instant counter culture classic.

Salena Godden, 2018

Two Little Ducks
(and Selected Poems
2015-2018)

Two Little Ducks

'Two Little Ducks' is a sequence of poems. It follows three narrative strands which alternate alongside each other, one poem at a time, before the final poem ties them all together. The concept was born in January 2017, with some pre-existing poems worked in or adapted slightly to satisfy the theme.

The first strand explores the core reasons behind so many working-class communities supporting Brexit. I grew up in a city which voted 66% Leave and find the sweeping "hothead Brexiteer" generalisation unfair. If anything, it only serves to deepen the mentality which led to the vote in the first place.

The second strand recalls my experiences volunteering at the Calais Jungle refugee camp, which I did either side of the EU referendum. I encounter an alarming level of anti-refugee sentiment both online and through conversations, and unfortunately there is an overlap with a lot of Leave voters.

The final strand uses kitchen-sink realism to tell the fictionalised story of a character called Maria. The character was born in summer 2008 and is referenced on both the second and third Skint & Demoralised albums. I've developed her story specifically to slot in with this piece.

Wake Up and Smell the Tetley's

Britain. The 24th of June, 2016.
Last night, at 9pm, I had a pencil in my hand.
Today, at 9am, I have a paper.
In twelve hours,
an earthquake left a chasm:

is it "Brussels-based Houdini"
or "Britain's Hari Kari"?

It's Winston Churchill's peace sign
and Liam Gallagher's bird.
The establishment deafened by
the voice they never heard.
A bulldog in the ballot box;
the table overturned.
A slingshot to the status quo:
a lesson truly learned.

It's the People's Revolution,
after decades disenfranchised
from the millionaires that tax us every day.
It's Cameron shuffling papers at the podium,
with his plastic smile cronies in dismay.

It's the working-class ecstatic
like I've never seen before.
Farage being hoisted up above
like Bobby Moore.
Crumbs of toast fall before
his gurning disbelief:
no seat in Parliament,
but right now, he's the chief.

See, the problem with elections is,
the government always wins:
all except this
precious referendum.
A pardon from the table
of an unelected club,
who kiss goodbye
to the trillions that we send 'em.

And it might have been
blind hope or
empty opportunity, but
why would anyone vote to stay like this?
'In' / 'Out', 'Leave' / 'Remain';
nothing in between.
They give us twos and threes
and then ask us 'Stick or Twist?'

Left behind and demonised:
we'd fight to stay afloat.
And we know they only give a shit
when they've given us a vote.
We're useful when we're cannon fodder;
a nuisance when we're not.
Project Fear; the people's pride:
a chance to stop the rot.

How dare they all campaign as one,
and beg us not to revolt?
Take an entire movement
with a massive pinch of salt?
Pin us all as ignorant,
fantasists and crooks;
where hope resides in scratch-cards
or 'Two Little Ducks'.

Shit on us,
for thirty years,
and then ask us for a favour.

Marvel when rebellion
presents a different flavour.
The bastards bleed us dry,
bridges slowly burn.
Work us to the bone,
nothing in return.

Too right
we chose to Leave:
it was tumbleweed or mystery.
Thunderstorms and fog;
or misty-eyed history.

A vote we could believe in.
An outcome we could cheer.
Vera Lynn on V-Day
and Vinnie Jones' sneer.

Whitehall trumped by Wetherspoon's.
The "Powerhouse" in the polls.
Wake up
and smell the Tetley's:
we've taken back
control.

(Of what?!)

Along the Tracks

It's the first weekend in August.
My weary feet trudge along the Calais concrete.
Razor wire wraps like a thorn bush,
on an endless stretch of electric fences.
Enamel signs that read:
"DANGER OF DEATH";
largely intended
for those who've fled warzones.

Items of clothing
are scattered like shrapnel.
Sleeping bags lay empty at roadsides.
I shudder, as I wonder,
how long they've been empty.

To my left-hand side is a port.
To my right-hand side is a motorway:
a road that's raised above rows of lorries
which slowly inch along.

The National Guard parked
on every roundabout.
Newspapers, aviators, guns and coffee.
Beads of sweat and scowls of suspicion.
You can almost smell the aftershave
as they strut around and spit on the pavement.
Their French cockerel versus my Fred Perry.

The landscape threatens circles.
My mind succumbs to doubt.
I've a phone bereft of data,
and a destination,
where I'm not supposed to go:

a "no man's land".
An eyesore of humanity.
A holding pen for desperate souls
with nightmares behind them,
and nothing in front.

"Ou es la Jungle?"
"Ou es la Jungle?"

With a final roll of the dice,
I find a road which curves with a railway track.
It's lined with trees and big grey boulders.
The boulders are around ten feet apart.
On three out of four,
there's a man sat staring:
across deserts, or borders, or oceans
of rubble.

I stop at the second man
(I bottled it at the first).
My awkward Yorkshire suffocates
the modicum of French
which has travelled with me twenty-two miles.

When I ask him a question,
it feels like a séance,
and I almost apologise
as he turns to reply.

He looks right through me
as I fidget through the silence,
and then he gestures to another soul
who's shuffling down the road.
Flip flops, and a rucksack
and a face
which speaks pages.

The sitter explains in a foreign tongue
and the shuffler nods
without pausing to process.

We walk, side by side.
There's a steady pace,
and the first words struggle,
as we strive to find parallels
beyond location and gender.
His ankles are weighed by shackles
which I'll never be able to see.

Call it "white liberal guilt"
or "checking my privilege"; but,
right now I feel awkward, and
angsty, and ashamed.

We walk, side by side.
I start to question why I'm here.
He's probably questioning why I'm here.
But really, deep down,
it's because neither of us get
why *he's* here.

We pass more lost souls
crouched on boulders.
And these pained brains all fix on borders.
And this British flag I'm born with
is a blessing and an imbalance,
and it's all these souls are yearning for
yet it views them all
as vermin.

But we walk, side by side.
In his rucksack, he has a sleeping bag:
like the one at the roadside.
As well as this, he has water, and papers.

He starts telling me how
back home, in Syria, he was a barber.
He took pride in his craft, and at 31,
his biggest concern
was how fast he's thinning.
We share a chuckle
as the Jungle emerges.

I'm greeted with the standard scene:
pushbikes, CS gas,
National Guard, London Calling,
volunteers, charred remains,
dead rats, barbed wire,
dusty rubble,
and deadly silence.

He goes to plot his next escape.
Last night they found him in the back of a lorry,
and tonight, he'll succeed, or he'll fail
or he'll die.

We shake hands
and then walk
in opposite directions
and all that we share

is the sky.

From Broadway to Bubbles

She's at the Broadway Launderette
in Blyth,
and it's Thursday the 5th of November,
but around here, every day
is the same.

It's a 21st century tumbleweed town;
Northumberland in slumber.
And this morning
they called her a moron, but
Maria
is her name.

Five days a week,
four types of coin,
three types of powder,
and both types of dirty laundry
(the dirtier, the better).

A conveyor belt for dignity
or dole queue for pittance.
A one-bed you can walk to,
or a two-bed in the sticks.

The sorry pathetic blunder
from the third machine on the left,
and then the symphony of silence
at 5.59.

Fifteen
hours'
freedom.

Maria limps down Newsham Road
with feet as sore as Sunday's head.
Obligation waits at home before
the haven of her bed.

Cheap cards on the mantelpiece
as sentiments are echoed;
the evening starts to lose its fizz
with the warming glass of prosecco.

The boyfriend leaves at 7
for the bonfire at the Quay,
leaving Maria sat
as mum starts to snore on the settee.

Sat stubbornly,
she smiles beneath the window.
Struggling to surrender any fucks.
Her solitary 22nd birthday:
the adulthood, of Two Little Ducks.

And she drifts between an evening
on the Bombay, and the blow.
Diluting her dilemma:
should she stay,
or should she go?

Farewell, Kellingley

(The original version was written when Kellingley Colliery closed on 18 December 2015. It was the last deep coal mine in Britain. I come from a line of coalminers on my dad's side.)

Every day as usual -
before the birds had cleared their throats -
he'd wake in a room dark as most ever see,
and creak to the kitchen:
four sugars,
in his pint of tea.

The deputy does not carry coal,
but a burden just as heavy.
He's to head in first
with his lamp and his nerve,
and satisfy his judgement

that without a single doubt to shirk
the pit is fit for lads to work.

Only, in those last days,
he need only be half awake;
as he trudged down a well worn path,
with the frame of the colliery
emerging as a silhouette.

No need to check the mine.
He wouldn't go past the picket.
But still, he'd have to phone his gaffer:
reporting in for vacant duty,
day in, day out, day in, day out;
just as usual.

Lads he loved like brothers,
after years of risking life and limb,
united on the picket line
where chance of work
was less than slim.

He'd to stand there and watch them:
either broken, or breaking,
or stone cold silent.

And they sent in all these coppers,
shipped in from elsewhere;
London, or Nottingham,
or somewhere else irrelevant.

And he could only watch in disgust
as they taunted the picketing miners;
wafting notes
that floated on laughter,
as though they were prodding
a caged-up animal.

It was so much more than a job
or a career.
It was his life
and his pride
and his honour.

Communities
and livelihoods
being torn apart before his eyes
by those employed to serve
and protect us.

To my Granddad, George,
it was on that day
that the mines closed forever.
This was no longer the industry
that our family could invest our lives in.

And thirty years later,
we've seen our final closure.
The fist that forced decline,
and the aftermath's exposure.

Hard drugs, hard luck;
voids left to rot.
People with nothing, but
they'll give you what they've got.

Thousands of lives
betrayed and abandoned.
Thousands of existences
struck off as stories.
Coal mines forever condemned.

Industries: in history books.
Prospects: a commute.
Postcodes left anonymous:
strangled at the roots.

I appreciate the pros and cons to coal.
But either way,
they acted with brutality.
Treated with contempt
and disregard.
Crushed by the state,
survive on solidarity.

Ideology that brought a generation to its knees.
Farewell, Kellingley.
Rest in peace.

Welcome To The Jungle

I expect to see
grown men with smartphones, sat in circles;
forging plans to smuggle into safety.
I don't expect to see a group of children playing football
on wasteland,
which had been housing thousands.

I expect to see despondency and despair.
I don't expect
smiling generosity.
Afghan naans, free of charge.
Empty boxes bringing beats.
I try to resist, but a penniless host
never admits defeat.

I expect to encounter some degree of
bitterness or jealousy, like...
I get my kicks from poverty,
and that's why I'm here.
I don't expect a group of homeless orphans
to greet a bag of cast-offs with a cheer.

Police patrol perimeters
with guns that need both hands,
beneath barbed-wire fences
that every language understands.
Barbed-wire fences
bought by taxpayers in Britain;
a message in a bottle
that doesn't need to be written.

Refugee Community Kitchen.
They've served over a million meals.
24/7, through volunteers
and donations.
But food comes third, with water first,
and smartphones sat in second.
You only survive through
constant communication.

I expect to see charities with gazebos.
I don't expect to hear
that they've been banned altogether.
And,
when men are found in lorries,
they confiscate their shoes:
left to walk on rough terrain
regardless of the weather.

I expect to feel mortified
and leave the place in tears, not
strangely reassured
as I walk away.
Hope, determination,
community and love,
all punctuate
a horseshoe of a day.

Jungle Book Kids Café;
the closest place to "home".
A cushion
for nearly a thousand kids.
78% of them
are living there alone:
the one stat
that my heart of hearts
forbids.

I end-up volunteering with a
group I meet from London.
Cleaning sinks and litter picking;
little stuff like that.
The refugees are humble,
and they thank us when we finish,
but,
you just feel like,
no matter what you do,
it could never be enough.

I was led to expect a rabid, hostile warzone.
Check my phone and my wallet
all the time.
But there's bookshops, barbers, theatres,
a boxing ring and a gym.
Some are institutionalised;
others,
entrepreneurs.

There's around twelve thousand people,
forced to flee from warzones;
crossing continents
to end-up living here.
But all I see on mainstream news
is "animals" and "tribes";
propaganda spiralling
xenophobic fear.

I arrive home
to the tabloids
still vomiting these names.
Call me a snowflake
all you want
but I feel thoroughly ashamed.

Hatchbacks & Lullabies

In the car park
by the Quayside,
as dark as it's gonna get,
hatchbacks are gathered
like the closing frames of snooker.
Girls giggle in harmony
with the odd nocturnal seagull,
and headlamps are a form
of winking from a distance.

Hotbox or hand-jobs or
simply passing time.
The juvenile adrenaline
that comes with petty crime.
Too young
or too broke
to try and chance it in the bars, so
Friday's misdemeanours
come in neon coloured cars.

This is where Maria met Ste.
She was 17, he was 23.
A Kermit coloured Clio
on a double date with Kirsty.
It's funny how,
the more you drink
the more it makes you thirsty.

Five years
and a fortnight
since he drove her back to his.

He promised her something special,
but, she's yet to discover what it is.

So...

She plans to just
let her hair grow
for a bit.
Use a £20 note as a bookmark
in her Sylvia Plath.
Let Stephen paint her toenails
as he watches 'Match of the Day',
and then stretch out
in her Pikachu onesie.

He makes the greatest brew on earth,
that boy:
two sugars and the shade
of orangutan whiskers.

They have to swim the channel
just to try and pay the rent.
A fortnight with a microscope
on every penny spent
before they plummet with the pressure
and its plundered by a drug:
a spliff instead of breakfast, or
red wine from a mug.

But with phones stuck in Flight Mode
and the doors double locked
there's nothing in the world
beats the comfort of this bubble.

And as Netflix babysits the bits
that drag and drift
between the shifts,
her eyes evade the calendar
and all she ever dreamt of.

Because,
it's easier to compromise
than pursue.
It's easier to accept
than to challenge.
It's easier to recalibrate
than to truly stick to your guns.

The last time she checked,
there was no parachute button
on the Virgin TiVo remote.

So...

She plans to just
let her hair grow,
for a bit.
And fall asleep with Sylvia
singing lullabies
from the page.

L20 1BG

*(This is an entirely factual account, which occurred in the
autumn preceding the EU referendum; during which the
Leave campaign pledged an extra £350m a week to the NHS)*

The rain beats down
on the windows of the car.
When you're lost, or you're late,
it sounds like chaos.
But when you're just fine,
and you're warm, and you're comfy,
it feels like someone's massaging your scalp
with the tips of their nails
on the tips of their fingers.

Thursday the 3rd of September.
You called by following a
routine check-up at the hospital,
shortly after 2pm.
I was upstairs, Lucy answered the door. Silence.
"You alright?" she asked. Silence.
"Matt, you'd better come down…" she said,
retreating to the kitchen, to the kettle.

And you looked straight at my chest,
with those Irish eyes, and said:
"I've got cancer."

The world slowly imploded
as I took you in my arms,
and we waited for the click

We sat and talked:
passing the diagnosis around the room
like a wailing baby,
trying to make sense of it,
and searching for calm.

Tuesday the 13th of October.
I called by,
following major surgery at the hospital,
shortly after 2pm.

They call them 'Gates' instead of 'Wards',
and it does look a bit like an airport,
but at least they had the heart
to avoid a 'Departure Lounge.'

You moved as though you were
standing underwater.
Spoke with the croak
of a young Alex Turner.
And as you shuffled towards me,
barefoot, in a night-gown,
I'd never seen anyone
looking quite that strong.

"You alright,
Mum?"

And you looked straight at my chest,
with those Irish eyes, and said:
"I'll be fine."

Thursday the 10th of December.
I called by,
following a Christmas gig,
shortly after 10pm.
We'd to dash via Agbrigg -
I'd forgotten my passport -
and then over the M62,
to the P&O Port at Liverpool.

With my phone drained of battery,
the Sat Nav took us to the wrong end
of the right port,
in complete darkness,
at 2am.
We tried asking a bloke by a lorry,
but he was a urinating
unilingual Latvian.

A frantic drive around Bootle,
rescued by the woman
in the all-night garage.
Terror,
and then tears,
and then panic,
and then relief.

The rain beats down
on the windows of the car.
When you're lost, or you're late,
it sounds like chaos.
But when you're just fine,
and you're warm, and you're comfy...
feels like someone's massaging your scalp
with the tips of their nails
on the tips of their fingers.

One-by-one,
the cars filter up the ramp.
The rain gives way
to echoes of engine noise:
waved on by conductors
in hi-vis jackets.

They feed us Fish & Chips
before bidding us good night.
At lights out,
I suck on an IPA,
and try reading Bukowski
by the light
from the fridge.

At this stage,
it just makes me feel tired
and inferior.

Instead, I sit watching you;
drifting off to sleep.
Your purple coat for a duvet.
A pillow from reception.
Peaceful as ever.

When we wake,
we'll be in Dublin,
where Irish eyes
are smiling.

God bless the NHS.

S.O.S.

Yesterday morning,
I complained to myself
about the person on the Megabus:
they were snoring
for five whole hours.

The lad beside me
counts himself lucky
that it took him three months to get here;
most of which spanning the Sahara Desert
in the boot of a car.

I told you about my heritage
and the coal mines.
Communities and cities
left sitting in reverse.

He told me about his moonlit flit;
no time to bid farewell.
Where cities
are left sitting
in rubble.

He's adopted this tranquillity
which can only be a shell.
A matter-of-fact complacency
from a year of "living in hell".

His neighbours have noticed.
Within fifteen minutes, curiosity
constructs circle.
It's like we're gathered around a campfire,
but its early afternoon,
and the sunshine helps a squint
conceal a grimace.

They see me as a beacon, or a telegram:
a vessel.
Each soul eager
that their story cross the border, because –
in their eyes – we'd rush to help
as soon as we knew the truth.

It's like
Auschwitz has a waiting room, or,
human beings are being graded
and these didn't make the cut.

They see Britain as being civilised:
it'll greet 'em with a hug.
But at worst, they'd meet revulsion:
at best, they'd meet a shrug.

They're not telling me things
to outdo each other. And,
I'm not telling you
to be a virtue signalling tosspot.

They're telling me
so that I go home
and shout it from the rooftops:
an S.O.S. from the final stage
of twelve-thousand journeys.

(They didn't know I was a poet, and I didn't know I'd write this show, but life works out like that sometimes).

One guy walked from Khartoum
to Libya.
Hundreds of miles, but
Google Maps says: "no route found".

I hear of boats built for twenty,
but filled with forty-five.
Or being chased away by guards with dogs
and hiding in the forest.

A fistful of berries for breakfast.
Witness to torture and rape.
Thousands of Euros to smugglers and guards;
anything to escape.

We've got Sudan, Darfur, Ethiopia;
Afghanistan, Syria, Iraq;
Libya, Yemen, Eritrea;
who'd rather *stay*
than even think of going back.

Totalitarian governments,
civil war and bombs,
compulsory conscription,
imprisonment
and murder.

Journeys swallow years;
swallow continents
and endurance.

And I crumble when their bloodshot eyes
beg
for reassurance.

Say You'll Be There

She'd prepared a pop-filled playlist
so they could walk hand in glove:
avoiding life's congestion
through the back streets of nostalgia.

Four years, and a hundred miles;
dual decades as distant strangers.
But still they manage to reminisce
on childhood's shared and sacred pleasures.

She remembers dancing
to 'Don't Stop' by S Club 7,
in the playing fields at St. Peter's
with Zoë's bouncing ginger perm.
He remembers rapping
to 'Re-Rewind' by Artful Dodger,
on the old abandoned railway track,
the final day of term.

It took two hours and twenty minutes,
but it was perfect.
When she finished
with the twilight of the afternoon to spare,
she contemplated filling in the label
with a gel pen.
It's his 29th birthday
which he's dreaded now for weeks,
but what better form of antidote,
than travelling back through time...?

She skipped her tea; too nervous to eat.
He'd said he'd be here at 7.

She knew it'd be closer to half past,
but at 6.15, she settled.
His decision now defining
her defiance
or delusion.

She passed the time with cigarettes
and neatly stacked the crap cassettes
and watched the clock and made a drink
and tried to sip it on the brink.
Checked her texts, checked again,
downed her drink, checked again;
tried to ring, but it rang right through;
tried again, but it didn't ring once.

"Welcome to the O2 messaging service for 07525364927."

She lingers by the mirror.
Leaves the voicemail sat recording.
Mascara halted in its tracks at 25-past 9.
Protected cheeks bereft of freckles,
hair no longer drawn by Disney,
but even with that wide-eyed wonder,
"where on God's earth is he?!"

Twenty years of wisdom
that should be there to guide her,
merely arrive in hindsight
whilst wounds are getting wider.

The bedroom waits with baited breath.
Her feet get cold,
so she rummages for socks.
A car pulls up:
through naivety comes nervous nausea,
but it's only Babs from 13B
in her taxi back from bingo.

Alone:
well versed, well masked,
and well past caring.

As she plays the final song,
for the fifth time in a row,
she aches to tiptoe down the hall
and crawl between her parents.
Longs for worries such as:

"Mrs Roberts set us homework
and I haven't done it yet,
and last time she made me stand up
in the middle of assembly.

How come my dad always pick me up from parties
before we've had jelly and ice cream?

And how come my school uniform
is plain, and maroon,
whilst the other kids have poster red,
with the school's name embroidered?"

Sink beneath the duvet.
Make a castle from the pillows.
As the Spice Girls sing a serenade
that resonates quite brutally.

A tentative request,
that echoes through a lifetime:
faithfully borrowed from 'Now! 36'
(Side 1, Track 1).

Say you'll be there...
Say you'll be there...
Say you'll be there...

I Matter

(Commissioned by York Arc Light in October 2014, and since adopted by Trinity Homeless Projects, for whom I've been an ambassador since summer 2015)

Now you see 'em.
Now you don't.

Now you see 'em.
Now you don't.

So, a suit wearing stranger slips in the street.
What do you do?
You check they're alright,
if there's anything you can do to help.
And you offer to call an ambulance,
and you buy 'em a bottle of water.
Do everything you can
to reach the Good Deed Feed.
And you see 'em off, and then carry on,
feeling snugly smug inside.
The smartphone buzzes
and the bus was on time:
all well and good.

But on the same street,
someone's slumped in a doorway.
A thousand-yard stare
and a warm can of
Oranjeboom 8.5.
A rolled-up cigarette
Last week's clothes.

Rather ironically,
what you might call "bed hair".

And they might mumble,
or they might well have conviction,
when they ask you for less than you left
in the tip jar at Costa.
Only this time, you don't stop,
or check they're alright.
And you know that there is something
you can do to help, but you carry on.
Blindly ignore 'em.
It's their fault, you think:
their choice.

But 50p
costs a whole lot more than acknowledgement
as a fellow human being.

Let me ask you something:
how many times do you see a homeless person with a dog,
and instinctively feel sorry for the dog?

And they say there's a system in place.
A system to help the homeless become "human again".
For these "inconvenient scourges on society".
But if you take someone
who sleeps in a doorway in the rain,
or in a barn covered in crawling rats,
or who shits themselves
with no fresh clothes;
whose life
is a never-ending 'Groundhog Day':
walking the streets again and again
but with nothing to gain,
except for the next meal,
the next drink, the next hit...

Christ alive,
do you really think
that they'd *choose* to turn back,
if the system
was anything like what it should be?
If the system was in place
to meet the needs of the people
who need it
more than you could even imagine...

Because they live in a parallel universe.
And the system might seem reasonable
within your expectations.
Keeping meetings at 2pm,
three weeks on Wednesday.
But this is a person who roams the streets 24/7.
Who's given up hope.
Given up trying.
And the system,
somehow,
has given up on them too.

If the people in place to help-out have given up,
how on earth do you expect these to even start?

When should vulnerability
ever meet blindly with disdain?
On this jolly game of Snakes & Ladders:
nine months of sacrifice and compliance,
one tiny blip, and it's back to the start again.
Why bother?

Some will fail, and maybe don't deserve a chance.
But for once,
allow them to enter a room as an equal.

And enjoy those simple words that everybody craves:
"I matter."

The Ghost

So, people do these "super shops".
They fill a car or a van
with whatever they can manage
and then drop it, Ad Hoc,
at The Jungle.

Nobody knows when their next meal is coming,
their next medicine,
their next sleeping bag or pair of shoes;
they just wait,
and make things last
for as long as they can.

April 2016, my first visit.

I see the back doors of a van fly open
to reveal stacks of fruit:
strawberries mainly,
but also oranges, apples, bananas...

You can imagine what that looked like in the crippling
        Calais heat,
when things are being rationed to such an extent.

News travels metres in milliseconds.
A hoard of children charge towards the van;
squeals of glee and desperation.

The bell before the six-week break;
a stack of gifts at Santa's Grotto;

a fleeting hand-out
of sweetness.

Now,
when riot police are managing crowds

they're told that

if over half-a-dozen people charge at once

they could be trying to incite a riot.

To an extent, I can understand that.

But when the people are children,

and they're charging towards fruit,

the deployment of CS Gas canisters

seems a tad disproportionate.

Eyes widen. Heels spin.
They flee as fast as they can.

The men wear helmets and shields;

the boys, only t-shirts and terror.

Unscathed eyelids barely bat.
The van is now invisible.

But as the canisters empty
in a vacuum of noise,
you can just about grasp on
the ghost of
the Gestapo.

Echoes From The Bottom Of A Well

Tonight belongs to these two,
and no-one else.
A bond that does backstrokes
through arteries.

Maria and Tanya.
Pizza and gin.
A friendship formed
in pigtails.

They privately survey their surroundings.
Assess the town with full panorama.
And Tanya always chuckles
when Maria pours the measures:
"that's meant to be a single?!
It's closer to a triple…"

Flashbacks and verdicts
are neatly interwoven,
with nicknames that would land them both
in *very* serious shit.

Maria dips her pizza in the mayo.
She used to dream of a townhouse
which overlooked a bay.
No need for seashells,
and a treat for young lungs.

She has sample pots from B&Q
in turquoise and magenta,
but lids gather dust
beneath a damp mushroom wall.
Lungs accustomed
to a different kind of moisture.

The lightbulb in the bathroom is flickering:
like an arm on the brink of wrestling defeat,
or canine eyes in the throes of sleep.

He's used the same towel for months on end.
The toaster keeps tripping the fuse,
and there's a Tupperware box in the top of the fridge
entirely filled with mould.

They laugh about the worst of times
and cry about the tiffs.

Each fresh scandal
is merely the council repainting the roads.

They arrive at the subject
that fills Maria with fear: Ste.
About how he ditched her
on her 22nd birthday.

Tanya laughs it off and says:
"Babe, you'll never top mine!"
and then soothes her with an anecdote
that springs from simpler times.

Tanya was kicked out on her 16th.
Maternal doors slamming
since the scuffle in the hot tub:
booze and blood and broken glass
erupting from the bubbles.

She spent three nights on the streets
and then nine months on sofas,
before her mother fell in love
and took her back.

Fish fingers,
Unwashed uniforms,
Candy Crush,
Krispy Kreme,

Amplified absences,
Leftover loaves and
Loathsome lovers.

Tanya sucks her fingers
when she's finished slicing lime,
as Maria briefly muses
on the love she's come to know.

Xbox, Netflix,
ready meals and tinnies.
Toenail clippings, ashtrays
and multipacks of crisps.

At 22 and 29,
they are busy waiting to die.
When she's alone, she feels horny.
When they have sex, she wants to cry.

She says that she's aching to leave, but,
the window of opportunity has passed.
Tanya says, "that's bollocks!"
and she pours another glass.

They swig, and they hug,
and they snigger, and they sigh,
and they sway to the old school bangers
(Fatboy Slim, Bassment Jaxx
and Madison Avenue).

They talk about
how utterly unfathomable it is
that either of them
will ever own a home.

About the threesome they had
on a holiday in Greece,

or how Tanya got pissed
with her driving instructor
when she passed
at the eighth attempt.

How,
of all the girls in their form group
when they left at Year 11,
there's only four of them
that don't have kids.

Babies born for benefits;
an "adorable escape".
Square pegs in round holes,
being battered out of shape.

They shake their heads
and smile
and then they revel in the silence.

Tanya falls asleep,
and Maria flashes a grin.
She fetches her a sleeping bag,
and then finishes the gin.

Red, White & Blue

The Britpop snarl. Geri's dress.
"Cool Britannia". "Girl Power".
Shaking hands with Tony Blair;
the nineties' finest hour.

Nick Griffin's BNP
from the ashes of the National Front.
The Falklands Wars,
"Up Yours, Delors",
the Boxing Day Hunt.

Contextual chameleon,
so keen to misconstrue.
Polarised reactions
to red, white and blue.

Winston Churchill, Austin Powers,
Michael Caine, Bouncing Bombs;
Rangers fans at Ibrox,
The Last Night of the Proms.

Flags beside the railway line,
Britannia Bar in Magaluf;
Northern Ireland's marching season...
soldiers sleeping rough.

This flag is liberal guilt
and pride and honour too.
An ever-crumbling Union:
red, white and blue.

It flaps and drapes,
emboldens, adorns;
comforts, confronts,
welcomes and warns;

verifies, intimidates,
emblazons, provokes;
for some, it's nostalgia,
for others, it chokes.

Mods or monarchy? Taint or teach?
Buckingham Palace or Benidorm beach?
Roadside burgers, Readers' Wives;
Enid Blyton's Famous Five.

Tourism, paraphernalia,
Boris Johnson's bumbling failure;
car stickers, calf tattoos,
coffins on the evening news.

A reg. plate on a lorry bound for Dover;
an orphan's eyes fixated at a tunnel by the port.
A victory lap for Team GB, that Sunday night in Stratford;
families nationwide, enraptured by a sport.

From 'Only Fools & Horses', "Corrie", and 'Mr Bean',
to the savage, brutal Empire,
and all that came between.

'The Great British Bake-Off'.
The crumbs of Enoch Powell.
Squinting for a lounger
in matching shorts and towel.

A pin badge on a polo shirt,
with braces, and a Harrington,
on a skinhead, in a flat-roofed pub.

A girl dressed in gingham
with a little plastic flag;
the Jubilee in sepia, in the local Liberal Club.

If it's an emoji in your Twitter name,
we probably disagree.
Bigots blurring boundaries:
should hate speech be free?

I feel bad for saying I'm ashamed of it.
I feel bad for saying I'm proud.
Arms aloft; chanting
with my back towards the crowd.

This flag is a threat.
This flag courts suspicion.
This flag is childhood
or chasing pole position.

This flag is my privilege.
This flag is my oppressor.
This flag is law and order.
This flag is an aggressor.

Yeah, this flag is kicking off
and this flag is clinging on.
This flag is a pensioner
that owns every swan.
This flag is liberal guilt,
and pride and honour too.
An ever-crumbling union:
red, white and blue.

Royal weddings, Fish & Chips,
Monty Python, Nelson's ships.
Swinging Sixties, Mersey Beat,
Dr Martens, Carnaby Street.

Who, Jam, Pistols, Stones,
Maiden, Oasis, Blur.
Henman Hill, the telephone;
"shaken, not stirred..."

Fry-ups in 40°c sunshine.
Cockney rhyming slang.
The Blackpool Illuminations.

In 1966, it was a symbol of the times.
Now, it's mainly racist connotations.

Oppressive rule in Ireland
for 800 years.
The invention of concentration camps.
Guns versus spears.

Rape, pillage, rule, ruin...
educate, transform.
Liberate from fascism.
Call migrants a "swarm".

The Butcher's Apron.
The Lonely Yomper.
Unification.
Divide and conquer.

This flag is liberal guilt,
and pride and honour too.
An ever-crumbling Union:

red, white and blue.

Le Tricolore

It's 5am in January
and the sky is like a mineshaft,
at the Jungle refugee camp
where sleep is at a premium.

They almost look like fireworks, but
they're heading for the ground:
these canisters of CS Gas;
designed to make you weep.

From the fog above a swamp
to a thick and creamy cloud.
By the dozen load
they're landing in the centre of the crowd.
Heartbeats quadruple
with the rockets' downward arc:
blue lights, white smoke, red sparks.

Folk disperse
like pool balls on a break,
as distant smartphones follow it like snipers.
Woolly hats and flip flops,
taking cover where they can.
The odd ironic cheer preceding chaos.

The National Guard are going hard
on unarmed refugees.
Ignoring shrieks of panic
and humanitarian pleas.
In riot gear,
they circle the perimeter like sharks:
blue lights, white smoke, red sparks.

Blinded bodies dodge between
grenades that cause concussion.
If they're lucky,
then the next lot
might land on that tarpaulin.
A well prepared assault
from the safety of the shadows;
no warning, no discussion,
no mercy.

Between businesses
and hand-built homes,
it suddenly feels like trenches.
Rubber bullets pummel flesh,
the water cannon drenches.
An air raid
in the dead of night:
just bites,
no barks.
Blue lights, white smoke, red sparks.

Blue lights.
White smoke.
Red sparks.

Tall Ships

There's a Tall Ships Regatta
in a couple of weeks.
She keeps spotting the posters in town,
all ClipArt and misplaced apostrophes.

She's loved them since she was a toddler.
Her old man would hoist her up,
and she'd ride on hairy shoulders,
gasping.

There's one at the Quayside now.
It's called the...
something da Vinci.
It might not be in the Regatta,
but its tall.

Behind it, the power station:
devoid of ambience in daylight.
In darkness,
it glows in honeycomb:
a looming presence at the Quayside.

(She prefers the place at night-time,
of course she does,
but on a sunny day like this,
it comes with irresistible charm).

She walks the planks, chuckling.
Dreams of diving in.
Like Ophelia,
she'd float on the oily surface,
between Morrison's bags
and seaweed.

Two spliffs in, she wonders:
if the wind turbines spun fast enough,
would they become propellers
and take Blyth to the moon...?

She smiles at swastikas
sprayed on the shutters
of the UKIP shop in town.
Despairs at schoolmates
stood queuing at the desk.

You can get to Newcastle city centre
in an hour on the bus,
but it's rare they ride further
than Whitley Bay.

Roundabouts and rituals;
comforts
and complacencies;
mind *under* matter.
Most days, she utterly loathes this town.
Apart
from the Tall Ships Regatta...

Voids Tempting Mischief

2005.
Labour are war criminals.
Blairism is rife.

The Live 8 concerts.
The riots in Edinburgh.
The G8 summit.

London is chosen
for 2012's Olympics,
and then the bombings...

Chaos ensues, as
Jean Charles de Menezes is
shot dead by The Met.

The threat of terror
lingers in the summer air.
Sound familiar?

I'm sixteen years old.
Government & Politics
at Sixth Form College.

Devil's advocate,
fuelled by rebellion;
passionate and proud.

I need a strong voice.
I need a sense of purpose.
I need an outlet.

A tumbleweed town;
identities abandoned:
voids tempting mischief.

'Quadrophenia'.
Mod targets and Union flags,
and teenage anger.

Leeds United games.
Bore draws in Division Two:
voids tempting mischief.

£2.20 pints
in my old man's shirt and shoes
at The Railway Club.

Fred Perry polo,
number one buzz cut, and a
Harrington jacket.

Passionate and proud,
but what's there to be proud of?
What do I cling to?

The Union Flag flaps
on bunting and in boozers,
and in history books.

We all know history
is written by the victors
in generous ink.

Up in Livingston,
there's a by-election swing
to the SNP.

Michael Howard goes,
and the Tories need a leader;
unknown Cameron wins.

Blair loses a vote
on the Terrorism Bill,
as tensions run high.

Sixth Form common room.
You either blend or rebel:
it is binary.

Individuals
thrive in the uncertainty:
voids tempting mischief.

It's not like before:
playground humiliation
in social quicksand.

Court controversy,
and the limelight will be yours;
and it's yours to own.

Leeds United games.
Coach trips around the country:
booze, flags and banter.

Blind drunk in Rotherham.
Frogmarched through
Burnley backstreets.
Bed-less in Cardiff.

Eight hours to Plymouth.
Winter nights topless in Crewe.
Blood-soaked in Sheffield.

And monkey noises,
as the coach snaked to Millwall.
Again, at Wigan.

Impressionable,
and caught up in the wrong crowd:
passionate and proud.

It starts on forums.
Dodgy links like dominos
bring propaganda.

And as you well know,
propaganda only works
when it's in disguise.

Eager to believe,
you start to delude yourself;
it's unstoppable.

Ideas excite,
common sense is abandoned;
you start to feel free.

Views clamed as your own;
instead of what you've been fed
by those up above.

Intoxicating;
that air of rebellion:
passionate and proud.

Blind to irony,
enraptured by defiance;
desperate and naïve.

An enamel badge
lands on the doorstep at home:
the BNP Youth.

When you feel oppressed,
you forget your privilege:
it's all relative.

There are no letters:
just a logo-based shape
of the Union Flag.

I stood, toe-to-toe,
with Holocaust deniers
and with hooligans.

I lie to my folks.
I don't admit what it is,
'cause deep down, I know.

A young white cis male
with dinner on the table;
a home with a roof.

But I wear it out.
Football games, even Sixth Form:
passionate and proud.

Obsessed with a flag.
The power of rejecting
all authority.

I align myself
with their vitriolic views:
voids tempting mischief.

The 'Dambusters' theme;
fists raised aloft in drizzle,
division unites.

I am not racist.
I am not homophobic.
I am not fascist.

And so there I went.
The crossroads of adulthood:
careering off course.

During the same spell,
in the Sixth Form common room,
I came out as bi.

A kick up the arse,
and a good old talking to:
I might be alright.

Passionate and proud,
destructive and deluded:
voids tempting mischief.

Twenty-Two Miles

Just twenty-two miles, that's all it is.
The sunlight bounces off the cliffs,
and because they're taller,
they look closer from France.

I listen to the waves,
lapping over breakfast.
I'd have a croissant and a coffee,
but I feel sick.

I'm sure if you've traversed
through continents and oceans,
you're gonna look across and think,
"I could swim that".

The seagulls float gracefully,
in ravenous packs.
And my head's a fucking shed
from all the parallels and chasms.

David Walliams: ten hours thirty-four. Sport Relief.
Eurostar: one hour. £29.
P+O Ferry: ninety minutes. £40.
Channel Tunnel: thirty-five minutes. £49.

A smuggler's dinghy,
in the dead of night:
up to £13,500.

Yesterday afternoon, I was sat playing cards
with Ethiopians and Eritreans.
The breeze picked up,
so they invited me inside:
into their home.

And no word of a lie, right,
no word of a life,
there was a Bradford City sleeping bag.
For those of you doing an internal shrug,
there are twenty-two miles
between my house,
and their stadium.

It's the same between Leeds and York.
Between Newcastle and Hartlepool.
Manchester and Blackburn.
Birmingham and Leamington Spa.
Northampton and Milton Keynes.
Oxford and Reading. Bristol and Newport.
Exeter and Torquay. Southend and Romford.
Portsmouth and Bognor Regis...
Calais and Dover.

They ask me, with wide eyes,
if Bradford are a decent team.
I haven't got the heart to tell the truth.

I want to ask them all how they got here:
how long it took, and how they managed.
But that kind of thing is either volunteered
or locked away.

They offer me a cigarette,
and I smoke it just to socialise.

I give them some Euros to buy some beers,
and I'm Father Christmas.

There are people who walked across deserts.
Whose drivers were shot in the chest.
Whose dinghies were sinking and floated ashore.
Whose bodies were subjected to unspeakable acts.

They burp with the beer
and cheer with the cards;
and for a while, it feels normal.
The universal language of betting and banter:
brotherhood forged in the belly of the beast.
Flags are now playful affiliation.

The lad sat beside me taps me on my knee,
so I lean in and lend him my ear.

He asks me very softly if I can justify
why *my* country
is leaving them here.

His question somehow silences the room.
Playing cards stripped suddenly of worth.
He's not asking me as a journalist
or a lawyer.
Just a fellow human being
on this earth.

I feel sick again,
with shards of sunlight
piercing through roof.

They ask me if they're likely
to be welcomed in by law,

and I haven't got the heart
to tell the truth.

It Wasn't Me

In the days before YouTube
(if you can imagine such a thing),
she'd head to HMV
to hear her favourite stars sing.
Queuing up for CD singles;
£2.99, and her stomach tingled.

She remembers one in particular.
'It Wasn't Me' by Shaggy;
featuring Ricardo 'Rik-Rok' Ducent.
There was a bonus feature,
and when you stuck it in the PC,
you could *watch the video*.
She didn't really get what the song was about,
but she liked it.

Probably still got in somewhere;
in the attic at her mum's.

Anyway,
she's at the Mecca Bingo
on Bridge Street.
She needs a single number
to win the house;
her right knee's tapping furiously.

"All the twos, twenty-two":
Two Little Ducks.
That's what she needs to hear.
Well, that's what she needs to hear right now, at least...

It's her 23rd birthday.
She's with Babs, from upstairs,
and Sheila: Babs' mate.
This time last year,
watching fireworks through the window:
abandoned at home by boyfriend Ste,
who went to watch the bonfire
with the lads at The Quay.

She's felt more like an old maid
with every week that's passed,
but in these towns you reach puberty
and your role is already cast.

Her right knee taps
and the dobber hovers
but the house is called.
A jubilant shriek from the corner of the hall,
and the psychedelic carpet
is inviting her to fall.
Babs heeds telepathy
and buys another gin.

She checks her phone,
and its zombified swiping,
through the chasm that grows
from two ticks to "typing".

Malicious rumours
in a WhatsApp group,
as certain as CCTV:
Ste, in an alley,
with Tina from the flats.
And he swears:
"It wasn't me.
It wasn't me…"

Not the Taste, But the Smell

When all your hopes
are pinned in Paddy Power.
Dreams fade in pastel coloured tower blocks
on the edge of town.
Cash flow, dictated by the hour.
And toddlers dragged from Boots to Greggs
are fluent in the frown.

I always voted Labour.
My parents did the same.
But ever since the nineties,
they were Tories by a different name.
Their councillors, callous.
Shoulders icy cold.
Spending millions on a palace, whilst
rising rent brings mice and mould.

The cost to ride Arriva from my pillow
to that stockroom
is almost worth an hour's working wage.
The rota holds me ransom.
Retail bleeds me dry.
Drama with our colleagues,
just to drift on by.

I always loved The Jockey:
no such thing as foes.
A triple house vodka
and a jukebox with The Pogues.
The dartboard on some chipboard, but
the wall resembled coral.
Whilst men abandoned wives, and then
lectured you on morals.
(It now provides pay day loans).

Most of us are in debt before we're twenty.
I've met alcoholics, who aren't even eighteen.
And those queues around corners
for Food Banks?
One of the most mortifying things
I've ever seen.

The postcode lottery:
skint and demoralised.
Year after year of being
politically colonised.

And there we had it: one vote
to shake it up forever.
Huge pockets of people
right at the end of their tether.

From Maradona's Hand of God
to Margaret Thatcher's fist:
it's not the taste of what we own,
it's the smell of what we miss.

The way my father's face would fall
when I asked him about the mines.
How pals of his were ostracised
for limping over picket lines.

How Orgreave and Hillsborough
were a message from the top.
After decades feeling powerless,
somehow, we've swapped...

It's a vote with *our* name on,
but there's toxic tar on the brush.
We can overthrow the overlords
that I campaign to crush, but...

This last few weeks have been rancid.
They've dragged it through the mire.
And I can't share a platform
with this xenophobic choir.

I cannot grant their racist jibes
with concrete validation.
A former city banker
who's bastardised the nation.

I've spent months indecisive.
I settled down with Leave.
Now?
It's nothing but a stain.

Hijacked by hatred,
racism and lies:
I can't live with myself
unless I vote Remain.

You saw what happened at sixteen.
Misguided and misinformed.

And when 'populist' movements
manipulate that...

don't say
we haven't been warned.

Where Is the Love?

When I look at faces in The Jungle,
they look back as though I'm a hologram.
A mirage in the desert.
A face in a cloud.
Someone they *think* they recognise
but can't remember why.
Broken repeatedly, bent on resolve.

When I look at newsstands in Britain,
I see "swarms", "imposters",
"criminals", "tribes",
"invasions" and "illegals".

I do not see "humans".
I do not see "victims".
I do not see love.
I do not see responsibility.

When I visit the school,
I meet Marco.
He's got a sofa now, in Newcastle,
but he's back and forth
like a boomerang.

He's a teacher,
a father figure,
a safety net
and a friend.

When I read of *thirty* children arriving,
instead of the *thousands*
that the Dubs Amendment allowed,
I see teenagers described as
"burly young men",
a demand for dental records,
and a narrative that paints them all as hooligans
and cheats.

They berate children for taking selfies at the Eurostar.
Enlarge pictures of them smiling
– circling their faces –
like to them, Britain is Alton Towers
(to be fair, it probably is).

When I ask about sleeping,
I hear of 4am police raids.
Tear gas in sleeping faces.
Blankets and shoes confiscated.
Sleeping bags sprayed,
rendered unusable.
Beaten with sticks 'til they run away:
barefoot, in the wet and cold.

When I watch the news,
I see refugees *usually* attacking lorries.
Lining the roads like a pack of wolves;
scaling fences
and sprinting towards Britain
(towards YOU!).

I see billboards consisting entirely of brown faces,
and a slogan that reads:
"BREAKING POINT."
It is remarkably similar
to the work of Josef Goebbels.

I see Britain First banners that read:
"FUCK REFUGEES,"
on demos where they bring knuckle dusters and hammers.

When I walk through The Jungle,
I pass a water tanker.
On the water tanker, there's some graffiti.
The graffiti reads:
"Where is the love?"

They won't find it in Westminster,
or most of the mainstream media,
or, rather alarmingly, a lot of the British public.

Now I'm not saying that everyone's innocent;
that every refugee is an angel.
But there's human crisis – right there –
and Britain is entirely complicit.
They're being terrorised, illegally,
by protective wings that we pay for.
Whilst all the while,
banning charities
and building bigger walls.

On the news, we see schemers and scroungers.
A million misunderstood.
Diverted, distracted and duped,
by a blindfold covered in blood.

You've got to ask yourself:
Why would they flee from home, leaving everything behind?
Why would they endure the journeys,
risking death in dismal discomfort?
Why would they settle in a camp
that's been described as "living in hell"?

And finally, as they rightly ask,
where is the love?

Time To Leave

The kind of thing that never happens
to people like them.
£2.2 million on the jackpot.
Ste's always getting on at her
for wasting money down at bingo,
but then he's dropping bin lids
on the Football Pools or Lotto.

Worst of all, it took him four days
to realise that he'd even won.
A packet of fags on Plessey Road
and a copy of The Sun.
Asking on the off-chance,
as foolish hope flickered,
and then he drowned in disbelief,
as the kids behind him bickered.

Ticket stuffed in wallet,
he walked out like Prince Naseem.
And what better way to celebrate
than cheering on your team?
A tenner at the turnstile,
and the clubhouse with a smirk.
Thomas Cook on Monday
instead of toiling away at work.

The rounds are his,
and soon the fizz is being passed about.
With news like this,
a Chinese whisper soon becomes a shout.
By 5 o'clock, he feels as though he's on his second pill:
a thirty-yard screamer,
as the Spartans win 1-0.

Maria finds him face-down in the bog.
He's thrown-up on his polo shirt:
he's a drunken blithering log.
She struggles to find a taxi
that'll give them both a lift,
and then she hears about his fortune,
and the evening takes a shift.

She verifies the ticket on his phone.
And then her throat fills with vomit
and she needs to be alone, so,
she runs on down to Broadway,
smokes outside the launderette.
The sun begins to vanish,
and her shadow casts a silhouette.

£2.2 million.
Think of the prison that could buy.
All needs catered for:
no excuse to fly.

So, she fiddles for a lighter,
and she takes the ticket out.
Her cheek allows a grimace
as her mind wrestles with doubt.

She's terrified of being alone,
but things can't stay the same.
Part numb, and part defiant,
she sets the thing aflame.

It curls up on the pavement.
Did she free, or did she thieve?
She turns her back on Broadway.
It's finally time
to Leave.

Two Little Ducks

We find solitary shoes on beaches
from a dinghy that's capsized.
Millions flee from Western bombs
and we all act surprised.
Meanwhile, on Fleet Street,
Nigel has his say.
A cock and balls on the cliffs of Dover:
"send them all away".

But as pints clink in Thanet,
they're beyond the brink in France.
We're "taking back control",
whilst they're aching for a chance...

And the gap between the things I've seen
on a TV screen and The Jungle,
is the gap between a certain stride
and a brow-beaten stumble.

A homeless orphan leaps
from a bridge to a lorry.
Communities and cities
are left sitting in reverse.

The Kurdish kid
on the Turkish shore;
a grain of sand in a quarry.

And every time we cast a vote,
we seem to make it worse.

In safe seats,
complacency is starting to erode.
Neglect that spreads between the blinks
like potholes in the road.
Deprive us of attention,
seduce us in campaigns;
as soon as that rosette's removed,
you tighten up the chains.

But there's hundreds of children
unaccompanied and afraid,
just twenty-two miles from our bubble.
A daily dance with death, to this
nightmare laden limbo.
Their cities are left sitting
in rubble.

Barbed wire on one side,
and Food Banks on the other.
Billionaires in the middle
pulling parliamentary strings.
It seems to me,
it barely takes a lifetime to discover,
that the voice of simple reason
is a bell that rarely rings.

And we've all these
"hothead, red top, Twitter Nazi,
Bulldog Brexiteers,"
but the majority of the Leave vote,
I'd class as social peers.
Down and out for decades
until democracy drove dissent.
I grew up in a city
that voted 66%.

I've seen boys naming teddies
after murdered sisters,
after parents spent their savings
to send them on a boat.
A teenage Eritrean girl
abandoned by police;
with cracked bloody feet,
and marks around her throat.

I've watched kids charge at strawberries,
and then flee from CS Gas,
after they've watched family members
being shot at close range.
Using debris from a broken fence
as a crutch for a broken leg,
after falling foul of a National Guard exchange.

For most, the scene will never change at all.
The market's on, the bins are out,
the bills are overdue.
We used to glide through decades, but
nowadays, we crawl.
"Remember when the globe was painted
red, white and blue?"

Apprenticeships are now weekend jobs
at JD Sports,
and the welfare state considers us a nuisance.

The view on the horizon
is fogging our thoughts,
and no-one seems to offer us translucence.

I know a lot of folk that blame Brexit
entirely on bigots.
And I know, from my heritage, that isn't fair.

But nothing that I've said
is any excuse for racism.
And I shouldn't need to say that, but,
it's real. It's there.

And if anyone goes on rants against refugees,
from headlines or red tops, or wherever...
from my miniscule experience
volunteering in France,
I'll hold aloft those stories
as a lifelong endeavour.

So, who do we blame for this mess?
The 52%, who opted to twist?
The victims of war, viewing Britain as bliss?
The Syrian barber;
Maria, who's acclimatised to bleak?
Or Michael Gove, who sang a tune
to reach his dizzy peak;
Boris Johnson, peddling lies
every time he speaks;
and EVERYONE
in the Remain campaign,
which was dismally fucking weak.

Kids in Britain are taught the meaning of poverty
without the need for books.
Kids in Calais are left to roam the streets,
or cling to the bottom of trucks.
Adults in power choose to turn their backs,
as the nation self-destructs ...

... My name is Matt Abbott,
and that was Two Little Ducks.

Selected Poems (2015-2018)

This is my début collection, so I really wanted to include the poems that I'd written during the same period of writing 'Two Little Ducks', as well as the piece itself.

There are a couple of snippets from these poems which were woven into 'Two Little Ducks'. In particular, 'The Yellow Bus', which was written after an evening working on a project with Foundation Futures. I took one of the factual accounts in this poem and worked it into the poem 'Echoes from the Bottom of a Well', with the character of Tanya taking on the story.

Except for 'Old Lungs, Young Lovers' and 'Hit Squad', these poems are all based on fact; capturing things that I've either personally experienced or directly witnessed.

The poems 'Slim Jim's Liquor Store' and 'Adjust the Brightness, Add a Filter and It All Seems Twice as Nice' recall experiences from when I first lived in London from 2008 to 2009.

The poem 'On Arrival in Ibiza on a Thursday in October' was originally published in Tim Wells' Rising zine in 2017.

The poem 'Sonnet for E Pellicci' was written in the café itself, and when Nev saw that I'd written it, he asked me to perform it to the whole place – which I did. He then did my breakfast at half-price, so I can't complain. If you've never eaten there, do so ASAP.

Overnight Megabus

Where denim and leather sit side by side
and strip-lights sabotage slumber.
Strangers stretching blurry eyed,
non-nocturnal minds encumbered.
Not through choice but desperate need:
the overnight Megabus, London to Leeds.

Where minutes match the miles on the motorway.
The strip-lights are surrendered,
leaving cricket scores in the Evening Standard
semi-censored by midnight's mask.
The old man squints,
with nothing but the Butterscotch glow
from Finchley Road
to illuminate his wickets.

Bare feet stick out in aisles.
It looks like a cross between a bingo hall
and a morgue on wheels.
The stuffy air stands
behind the shoulders of your lungs,
forcing them to work for every breath.

The toilet
is out of order.
The stench floats just above your nose,
like the Baileys in a Baby Guinness.
Whenever you lean back to rest your head
(which is fairly often at 2am),
it cackles and catches you unaware.

And then you snooze for a bit,
with jacket between head and shoulder.
Trick your brain into thinking there's a duvet and a mattress,
until the booze morphs a mouth
that's munched a month's worth of crackers.

The hot air stifles and your forehead pounds,
but still...
three quid from London to Leeds!

Look around: we're winning at life.
We drop off at Rugby, and Leicester,
and Loughborough and Sheffield.

Sunlight creeps like a magnifying glass
on a coach full of ants
being dragged from the capital.

The particles of shit from the blocked-up bog
form a Morris dance pattern 'round your nostrils.
The Services are always twenty-five miles away.
Jesus still loves us.
This billboard is still FOR SALE.

The cricket scores in the Evening Standard
have fallen to the floor.
The picture of the crease all creased by his sandals.
The strip-lights fight for attention,
but they're long since a formality.

The overnight Megabus. London to Leeds.

Blurry eyes now bloodshot.
Strangers carry awkward familiarity.
Snoring and sighs, stretches and yawns:
cash is the Queen,
and we
are the Pawns.

Slim Jim's Liquor Store

Slim Jim's Liquor Store:
a "masterful purveyor of good times,"
by all accounts.

A jukebox bar,
with red cracked leather stools,
old brick walls
and neon lightning.

A young rock-star
with dread stacked
never fools
the boys with the bottles,
and all required remedies.

Bras on the ceiling
exchanged for the fizz.
An open-door policy
to all who like it
hard and fast.

Far from the feeling,
strange though it is,
that down those darkened steps
outside
is Islington, 2009.

During that last hour of CBT
you were played three times
by the BBC.
And texts fly through
to a phone on the blink,
as the Tiger greets
the afternoon departure.

An awkward glance
from your housemate Chris
says it's far too soon
for the Bombay bliss;
a perplexed sigh soon says
"let the fucker drink",
amidst wider scenes
of determined debauchery.

Hours pass by and the mood improves.
Don't try and talk to the women in the booth;
you're on Jim's time now,
this is voluntary confinement:
collisions with reality
are always best at bay.

'L.A. Woman', 'Light My Fire',
play it dumb and fight desire;
'Back Door Man', 'Break On Through',
Mr Mojo may construe...

No natural light,
no clocks: no clue.
A finger down the throat
says you'll last 'til two.
'Back Door Man', 'Break On Through',
Mr Mojo may construe...

A wallet stuffed
with customer copies
of card receipts.
A clammy forehead.
Eight missed calls.

Slim Jim:
a masterful purveyor
of good times...
...the best.

Between Subbuteo Fixtures

Hidden in the attic,
as though the referees wore 'Bernard's Watch';
Subbuteo heroes
await on tenterhooks.
Reporter's notepads at the ready;
team-sheets scribbled in Period 5,
when I should've been taking homework.
Alien Ant Farm on cassette, on repeat
(the original 'Smooth Criminal' to untrained ears),
and my Nokia 3210.

Sammi confirmed that Gemma said "yes"
from the opposite side of the court.
Wimbledon hooked everyone that summer.
Subbuteo subbed for backhand swings.
With hands that read:
"Gemma 'n' Matty 4eva",
in scented pen.
With hands shrivelled by sweat
throughout 'Tomb Raider'
at Cineworld.
Neither knowing when
to let go.

The pranks calls ceased on the landline.
You'd always let it ring twice,
so that nobody picked up,
but knowing I'd always call back.
A few dates postponed. Subbuteo resumed.
And then a text, on the 3210,
in injury time.
"I'm dumping you for James Thompson."
We'd lasted seven days.

Mind the Gap

A 100m pulse race down the platform:
switching carriages
for strength in numbers
at Bootle Oriel Road.
Seven boys. Seven girls.
Mismatched, but slowly adjusting.

"Am I hurting you?" she asks,
at Bootle New Strand,
as she tentatively perches
on knees brimming with pride.
"No way," he asserts,
with cheeks still flushed.

It could be all the way to Southport,
or across to San Francisco;
his knees will never falter
whilst others catch their breaths.
His coat: Lyle & Scott.
Her scent: Gucci Rush.
His hand, on her thigh,
at Waterloo, retreating to a brush.

To them, at 26,
I am just another adult.
A world away from their parents,
yet a world away from their peers:
merely miscellaneous
amidst mischievous.

As I stand to leave, at Blundellsands & Crosby,
I notice his knees trembling.
A knowing smile as I step into the drizzle:
twelve years, and none the wiser.

Adjust the Brightness, Add a Filter, and It All Seems Twice as Nice

I never gave you my address,
but you knew I lived in Islington.
I'd mentioned a few times
that I loved The Lord Clyde,
so I must be this end of Essex Road.

There were folk I saw daily
on that little stretch.

The old guy at William Hill,
who'd beg for change with a bowler hat.
He'd bet on West Indies in the cricket, or,
whichever nag took his fancy, or,
how many throw-ins there'd be
during the first half
of Saturday's 12.30 kick-off.
That was late morning.

Late afternoon,
the woman smoking outside the launderette;
in pastel coloured t-shirts,
three quarter length leggings,
and Hi-Tec trainers.
She always looked like she was waiting for something,
and yet she knew it'd never happen.

Late night, the guys in Essex Road Kebab.
Same order, never spoken:
large chips and mayo,
to match four cans for a fiver
from the mini mart next door.

Every day, give or take, whenever home
from the road.
Never expected, but always just
there.

We would all decorate and arrange
our own forms of loneliness,
with varying degrees of futility,
and various types of filter.

Safe to say,
when I saw you by the door in Sainsbury's Local,
it was far from expected,
and far from routine.

You'd travelled down on a summer morning,
purely on the off chance that you'd see me.
You knew I had the day off:
we'd been texting 'til 2.

My usual routine involved
something on toast at half past ten,
and then a can of Gin & Tonic
before The Clyde opened at 11.

But you'd travelled down, specifically,
on the off chance that you'd see me.

And as we cut across, towards Upper Street,
I'm not phased, and I'm not disturbed.
Except only that,
The New Rose doesn't open until 11 o'clock either.

We turn left, pass Slim Jim's,
and down towards Angel.
The York
is open,
and in the sunshine, you oblige.

A double Bombay and a slimline
carries shifting connotations:
but acceptable in pairs
at this side of noon.

You wince, push away your glass,
and ask me for a single.
I tell you I'll do a swap,
but sink it straight down at the bar.

We catch the Northern line to King's Cross,
then the Piccadilly to Covent Garden.
We stroll down the Embankment
toward the face of Big Ben.
Pass Parliament Square,
where placards speak only
to tourists.

Through the back streets of Westminster;
just drifting, barely talking.
Well aware that: the tone of your visit,
and the ease of my welcome,
does not go a very long way
for respective stabilities.

We drink in a pub called The Speaker.
As the gin takes its toll,
you use the Gents' loo by mistake.

Eventually, you fall asleep,
by the fountain at the Palace,

and leave me,
not to question,
but to revel in
the opposite.

Ferrybridge Services

Sat slurping black coffee
in the services, gone midnight.
You almost kid yourself it's cinematic,
as lorries fly by in the inside lane:
blurring with the reflections
from the seats by the window.

Premier League highlights
on the plasma in the corner
probably would've been omitted
from anything cinematic.

Ferrybridge Services,
from the inside, looking out.
When you were younger,
you and your mates could see this spot;
watching down from the Warwick estate,
as analogue eyes sought mischief.

Dialling 999, reporting bombs,
and then waiting for patrol cars
to frantically soothe your boredom.

So, if this is cinematic,
I guess Shane Meadows might call the shots.
"Sing us some more sink estate sonnets!"
before a lingering frame
on your soya milk latté.

Fiddling with your Dockers,
scowling at the boom mic
and silently rolling a cigarette,
whilst West Bromwich Albion
celebrate in the background.

On Arrival in Ibiza on a Thursday in October

It's 1am, and I'm outside a café
in shorts and t-shirt.
I circle in the road towards a shuffled approach.

The gentleman inside...
he has the spitting image of a John Smith's belly
and a 'tache that'd fare well at darts.
He saunters across the tiles
and then starts collecting menus.

I enquire
– half English, half Spanish –
and he welcomes
– half smiling, half sighing –
and in walking towards the service point,
he beckons me inside.

In all his weary nights,
I bet he never deemed this poetic.

Aside from two locals on Coca-Cola,
I'm the only punter in sight.

I widen my eyes for a nod of approval
to reach inside the fridge:
grasping a beer,
and 1.5l of water.

The bartender sails across her freshly swept tiles
before leaning towards tiptoes
at the till.
I speak in Spanish,
and she responds in English.
This trend is never broken.

I gaze into the neon
as I suck on my Corona:
this morning I woke up in Grimsby, so,
I'm struggling to adjust.

Black ashtrays,
white tables,
black chairs
and silent streets.

I manage to earwig
about five percent of their conversation.
I'm pretty sure
they're slagging off the chef.

But as the hombre lobs his towel
over his shoulder,
the bartender hums to Manu Chao
as she skirts back over the tiles,
and I slowly peel the label
from my bottle:

all three of us are united,
and utterly alone,
in the most comfortable of silences
I think I've ever known.

Midnight, Leeds Coach Station

It's only midnight, but it feels much later.
Leeds coach station:
less for lost souls, and more for rejected reels.
A man whose "s" makes a whistle
is demanding to go to Rotherham.
Meadowhall, five miles down the road,
will not suffice.
An Asian woman circles the perimeter:
chuntering to herself beneath the mist-like drizzle
as she waits for the 465.
Arguments ensue over the ticket machine.
I offer a sympathetic smile to the lime green tabard,
who raises his eyebrows in response.
He allows himself a smirk
as eyes slip out of contact,
before it's back to the barrage
from Rotherham.
The coach to Meadowhall is at 00:20.
The coach to Rotherham is at 02:20.
Meadowhall is maybe a £10 taxi away,
or an hour's walk,
but he's insistent on direct travel.
My ticket to Wakefield cost £1.90.
My Tunnock's caramel wafer cost £1.00.
The Asian woman checks the time again.
It hasn't changed.
Off she chunters:
exchanging dialogue with the midnight air.
Another new shopping centre,
pregnant above. The Playhouse snoozes.
A trio of taxis contemplate turning in:
too expensive for this life.
The cash machine is out of order.
The toilet is 30p.

The city looks like a screensaver,
but the sound of machinery
grunts from the shadows.
Mr Rotherham lights a cigarette by Bay 1.
He is not told to put it out.
Lime green tabard takes a carrier
to his navy Vauxhall Zafira.
The bag looks cheaper than 5p.
The machinery makes a dim ringing sound:
throbbing in the breeze.
On its arrival,
Mr Rotherham attempts to board the 465,
for which he did not purchase a ticket.
He pushes to the front of the queue.
You can't buy tickets on board.
The closest stop
is Sheffield city centre.
He throws down his cigarette;
unsatisfied with the distance.
The man in front of me
is travelling to Budapest.
I'm travelling 10.6 miles,
although I did start the morning
in Calais.
In a coffee shop in Euston,
I read 'Howl'.
I worked through it slowly,
repeating each stanza.
I still don't understand it,
but I like it much better.
The woman beside me
orders a taxi from Mansfield.
The reading light does not work.
This coach does not carry
wandering souls,
but rejected reels.
Some are between auditions.
Some will never be seen.

The Yellow Bus

*(Written after an evening spent working on a project with
Foudation Futures, and entirely factual)*

Blacked-out windows on the battered yellow bus
may prevent pedestrians from scrunching up their noses.
But for these girls, those scrunches
are merely the soundtrack.

Air strikes launched on the dashboard:
clumps of padding from the backs of the chairs
bouncing off the windscreen,
and nestling in the foot well.
A few foam missiles
aren't much to have to deal with,
but when the air strikes are constant,
it becomes a different matter.

Mid evening in mid-August.
Sunlight glares on the bonnets that we pass.
"Left before the lights,
and then pull over by the Off Licence."
Another passenger for the yellow bus
climbs aboard and flashes a smile.

We snake through the pebbledash estates.
We're in the suburbs of Newcastle,
but at this stage it's anonymous:
Byker kids in Barça kits,
paddling pools and Union Flags.
Radio 1 cranked up to eleven.
A three-point turn in a cul-de-sac.
Snapchat making animals of adults unaware,
and Amber Leaf being passed about
as air strikes reach a ceasefire.

One of the girls on board
was kicked out on her 16th birthday.
Maternal doors slamming
since the scuffle in the hot tub:
booze and blood and broken glass
erupting from the bubbles.

The last thing that she saw,
as she peered over her shoulder,
was her tiny toddler sister
with her hands against the glass.
She could've done with the cash from babysitting
since they turned her down at Aldi.
She's old enough to fend for herself,
but her little sister's helpless.
Destined for evenings filled with:

Fish fingers,
Unwashed uniforms,
Candy Crush,
Krispy Kreme,

Amplified absences,
Leftover loaves and
Loathsome lovers.

But the atmosphere brings giggled gossip.
The news isn't treated as traumatic.
And the girls take turns, exchanging tales:
blissfully unaware of any scrunching.

The yellow bus backs into a space,
and sunlight dances on the North Shields quay.
The air around us is deadly still
as we step down to the concrete.

They head off in pairs.
You might think they're conspiring,
but mainly they're confiding.
Cigarette smoke rises
above every single missile
that's been bouncing off their windscreens
for as long as they can remember.

I look around me.
I see six remarkable young women.
I hear six voices eager
with ambition and resilience.
I hear six tales, matter-of-fact,
and *that's* when I scrunch up my nose.

They're left to live and learn
in limbo.
Bars on windows,
padlocks on doors,
and paint that peels
amidst patches of damp.

Bereft of any sense of value.
Left without an open door.
Theft of a level playing field.

A system that's stacked
for square pegs
in square holes,
square lives
and set roles.

Being average is a blessing.
Being normal is a virtue.
Being left behind is a one-way street,
and the postcode lottery
is a simple fact of life.

But they finish their fags,
flick through their filters,
and for the three hours that follow,
they fill a room
with laughter.

It's infectious at the time,
but the streetlights blur with a tear.
First you hear hyenas,
then you see hedgehogs.
Limbs masked by Adidas
which quiver with anxiety.
These girls present potential
that's been strangled at the source.
Fuck me, it's frustrating.
A generation gargled.
And one-by-one, they wave goodbye
to the battered yellow bus.

*(Around six weeks after that night, Foundation Futures held a
fundraiser at The Sage in Gateshead. They managed to raise
around £15k for a replacement to the yellow bus, which made a huge
difference as you can imagine. You can learn more about their work
at foundationfutures.org.uk)*

Keepy-Uppy

Six lads standing in a carousel.
An impromptu stage beside Bella Italia.
Raven coloured blazers,
a tangerine football,
and audience from pensioners
to prepubescent.

They juggle the ball in scuffed shoes.
It zig zags around the circle.
Textbooks in rucksacks are a pitiful challenge
beside keeping that ball
from that concrete.
One fringe rock hard with gel,
beside an afro which bounces like candy floss.

I watch them, transfixed, at 28-years-old.
I'm wearing size eleven Dockers and I'm carrying a bag,
but I still feel my right leg twitching.

There's a gaggle of girls by a bench:
no doubt heaping pressure on the boy that's in possession.
They're filming on Snapchat and giggling behind fingers;
eager to be impressed, as the crowd starts to swell.

Inches punctuate elbows,
as shoppers jostle for position,
and one man in particular
summons my attention.
The way he watches that football,
as though it's a pianist or a ballerina.

His walking stick, with the rhythm of the kicks,
tapping on the precinct.
His afro grey and thinning on top.

Crows' feet and wrinkles,
but his eyes belie his age:
he's vicariously guzzling
at the fountain of youth.

The crowd begins to cheer with every kick.
Faces contort with concentration.
Beads of sweat begin to trickle,
before they're joined
by a shirtless youth.

He bounds into the centre,
boots the ball
high and mighty,
and then bows
to the boos.

Gurning and foolish,
he's shattered something beautiful.
Turquoise bus, 1.
Tangerine ball, 0.

Old Lungs, Young Lovers

In flat roofed pubs on the corners of estates,
he clutches his carrier with pride.
They have the lyrics on the screen,
but this man is analogue:
typed up, stacked neatly,
and then despatched into plastic.

He winces as he watches young romantics;
cavorting, and dancing at angles.
Nursing half a Theakston's until the karaoke resumes:
his Sunstar   spotlight.

His voice is gravelly nowadays -
with a croak as he pushes his range -
but twenty years previous,
this guy was a different class.

Eyes scrunched,
he serenades the lovers that escaped,
as the young romantics fumble through
the food of distant dreams.
Dumb to what they're missing,
and how precious these moments are.

His three minutes flash,
and he picks up his bag,
and he shuffles to his stool at the bar.

Glen Campbell. Johnnie Walker. Tom Jones.
And then bed.

Old lungs. Young lovers.
Every Friday,
from 8.

The Swan Lake Shuffle

To focus on his hands
there might be strings of a harp or
fingers attempting to thaw.
But playing cards leap
like bingo balls or acrobats:
the jarring of the carriage
doing nothing to dissuade him.

His face spells numb disengagement.
Vacancy suggesting
he's unoccupied for hours.
But his digits and that deck
dance with all the grace of Glasgow,
and like dominos he captivates us;
one-by-one
from smartphone screen.

Heads bob
on a Subway train contained by silence.
He's oblivious
to the dumbstruck looks
from the passengers surrounding.
I almost take a picture, but,
a poem serves him better.

He escapes us at St. Enoch's,
as the strip-lights start to flicker.
Pupils return to pixels:
his bear seat sagging.

An audience left hungry on a Thursday afternoon.
Cards sitting static,
until he plays another tune.

Sonnet for E Pellicci

A Cockney-Italian concoction.
This century old snug on Bethnal Green Road.
Woe betide you take the veggie option:
tongue tucked in cheek, at this family abode.

Men betray their roots with cappuccino;
find solace from the city's morning rush.
Others flick through papers like a Beano,
whilst banter brings you breakfast with a blush.

Jessie Wallace beams above the punters.
Millennials on mobiles keep it schtum.
Neville makes you chuckle as he chunters.
Anna, gliding and smiling as she hums.

Warm as a jacuzzi, sharp as a knife:
Pellicci's; preserving East London life.

Hit Squad

The squad are out in force today.
It's barely noon and already I've seen three
out of five.

A brown envelope for a crimson puddle
beneath the ever-inviting sky:
cotton wool the shape of camels
swimming through a penthouse pool.

I don't recall which one I paid.
Night black as fetish leather;
stars refusing to watch.

This quintet of strangers
stalking anonymous streets
piercing the monotony
of predictable routine.

Each role entirely inverted
with the imminent threat
of eternal silence.

Mortality sold to a flashing moment
which lines the pavements
with a devious thrill.

Which one will it be,
and when?

But now,
the days feel much lighter
as the clock ticks much louder.

A brown envelope for a crimson puddle
beneath the ever-inviting sky.

Socialist Saliva

Don't let 'em tell you the NHS
is destined to be privatised,
dump you in a global recession
and force you to acclimatise;
moralistic platitudes
when Parliament's alive with lies.
t'old Murdoch'll be laughing
on the day democracy dies.

From benefit cuts to the Bedroom Tax
we return to:
"no Irish, dogs or blacks".
'Immigration Street',
"yeah, let's kick 'em out,
and boot 'em 'ard!"
What about 'Tax Evasion Terrace',
'Banker's Bonus Boulevard'?

I'm sick to death of bankers for bosses;
billionaires inflicting losses
on working folk
who are skint and demoralised,
year after year
of being politically colonised...

Don't let the Tories inflict any more.
They might've won the battle,
but we'll win the war.

Over the next five years,
the art of protest must be mastered:
if we all spit together,
we can drown the set of bastards!

THANK YOU

I owe a great deal to my mum, Jan, and would also like to thank my sister, Rosa, and my dad, Simon. I'm very lucky to have them.

David Gledhill took me under his wing when we first met in spring 2007. He introduced me to The Smiths, encouraged me to listen to Bob Dylan, and then wrote the musical backing for the demos which landed S&D a major record deal. He's been my best pal ever since.

Steve Larnach championed S&D from the off and was largely responsible for the record deal. He still champions me now. Christopher Morse gave both me and S&D our first ever gigs.

Since returning to poetry in 2013, I owe an awful lot to promoters including Pete Eastwood, Choque Hosein, Penny Sanders and Dean Freeman. A special shout-out to Crispin Flintoff and Francesca Martinez for the Stand Up For Labour gigs.

I owe a colossal thank you to Michael Bolger, who runs The Poetry Takeaway. This man has played a significant role in completely transforming my life, in more ways than one (#LoveYourWork).

I'd like to thank Louise Fazackerley, Toria Garbutt, Salena Godden and Jack Simpson for their partnership on Nymphs & Thugs, plus Mick Scholefield and Martin Colclough from Heist Or Hit Records.

Thanks to Pasco-Q Kevlin for giving me the confidence, to Stuart Bartholomew for publishing me, and to Jacqui Wicks, Caroline Rountree and Rob Reed for the laughter and support.

Thanks to Sally Kincaid and Leda Cashman for taking me to The Jungle in April 2016, and especially to Leda for stopping the French border police from shooting me on the way back (genuinely).

And finally, to Maria Louise Ferguson — my absolute world. I love you more than Blyth Spartans and The Labour Party combined.

ABOUT VERVE POETRY PRESS

Verve Poetry Press is a new press focussing initially on meeting a local need in Birmingham - a need for the vibrant poetry scene here in Brum to find a way to present itself to the poetry world via publication. Co-founded by Stuart Bartholomew and Amerah Saleh, it will be publishing poets this year from all corners of the city - poets that represent the city's varied and energetic qualities and will communicate its many poetic stories. Look out in 2018 for stunning first collections from Amerah, Casey Bailey, Leon Priestnall, Nafeesa Hamid, Rupinder Kaur, Kamil Mahmood and Hannah Swings.

We will also look to help poets from further afield who have supported or featured at Verve Poetry Festival and who we feel it is important to get into print. Matt Abbott falls into this category. The Nymphs and Thugs Showcase event he produced for us at Verve 18 was fabulous. And now we are thrilled to be able to help *Two Little Ducks* land with the explosion it deserves to. It is an honour to work with him.

Like the festival, our press will strive to think about poetry in inclusive ways and embrace the multiplicity of approaches towards this glorious art.

Keep an eye on what we are up to! Join our mailing list at https://vervepoetrypress.com/mailing-list

https://vervepoetrypress.com
@VervePoetryPres
mail@vervepoetrypress.com